MATTHEW

This Book Is A Gift From

Wilton Library Assoc.

Every child
needs a little
T.L.C.!

T.L.C.

THE LITERATE CHILD BOOK CLUB

A Harwich Junior Women's Club Project

Some Plants Have Funny Names

by Diana Harding Cross
illustrated by Jan Brett

CROWN PUBLISHERS, INC.
NEW YORK

For John and little Roo

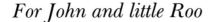

Text copyright © 1983 by Diana Harding Cross
Illustrations copyright © 1983 by Jan Brett
Manufactured in the United States of America
Published simultaneously in Canada by General Publishing Company Limited
10 9 8 7 6 5 4 3 2 1

Library of Congress Cataloging in Publication Data
Cross, Diana Harding.
  Some plants have funny names.
  Summary: Delves into the origin of unusual names
given to plants growing in the woods, fields, marshes,
and along streams and roads of North America. Includes
drawings of plants such as cattails, lady's slipper,
and Indian paintbrush in their natural setting.
  1. Plant names, Popular—North America—Juvenile
literature. [1. Plant names, Popular] I. Brett, Jan,
1949–   ill. II. Title.
QK13.C8 1983 581'.014 82-23438
ISBN 0-517-54840-2

The text of this book is set in 18 point Baskerville.
The illustrations are line drawings, with half-tone overlays,
prepared by the artist, for black and red.

Contents

Some plants have funny names.
Many were named
for the way they look.
Others were named
for what they do.
Still others were named
for where they grow.
Some plants were named
so long ago,
no one remembers
how they got their names.
But knowing the name
of a plant
may tell you something
about it.

4

5

All the plants
in this book
can be found growing
in the woods, fields, marshes,
or along the streams and roads
of North America.

JACK-IN-THE-PULPIT

Jack-in-the-pulpit
is one plant
that was named for
how it looks.

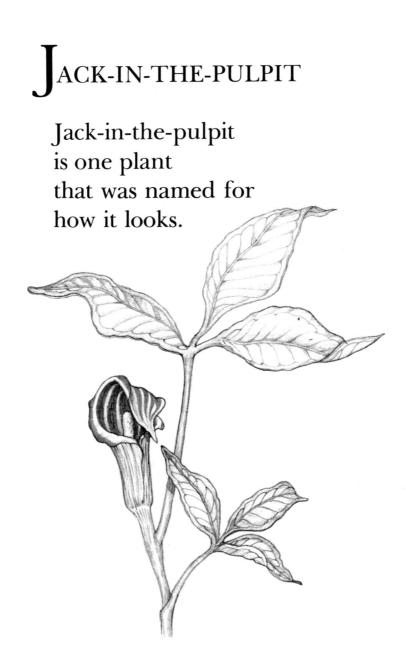

Peek under
the brown-striped hood.
Part of the plant
sticks up inside.
It looks like a little man
standing up to preach
in his own little church.
That is how the plant
got its name.
Jack-in-the-pulpit
is found in wet woods
in the spring.

9

LADY'S-SLIPPER

This pretty flower
looks like a
lady's shoe,
and therefore it is called
lady's-slipper, or moccasin flower.
Some lady's-slippers are yellow;
others are pink and white.

11

Look for them
in wet, shady woods.
But if you find one,
leave it there!
Lady's-slippers are very rare.

Bloodroot

If you break the stem or root
of a bloodroot,
you will see
how it got its name.
The red juice of this plant
looks like blood.
Indians used the juice
for face paint.
Bloodroot has a pretty
white and yellow flower
and big green leaves.

15

The first leaf to unfold
helps protect the new bud
as it pushes through the snow
in early spring.
Clumps of bloodroot
are found along the roads
and in the woods
of the eastern United States.

CATTAIL

The cattail is another plant
named for its looks.
Some people think
the fuzzy brown spike
at the top of this plant
looks like a cat's tail.
This fuzzy spike
is full of seeds.
In the fall
the cattail splits open,
and the seeds blow away.
Some seeds will land in the mud,
and new cattails will grow there.

19

Cattails are found
near the edges of ponds
and in swampy places
all over the country.

21

MILKWEED

Break the stem
of a milkweed plant.
A creamy white liquid
will ooze out.
It looks like milk,
but it really isn't.
But it does tell us
how milkweed got its name.
Look closely,
and you may see
caterpillars
feeding on the milkweed leaves.

23

In late summer
the milkweed pods
are full of silken seeds.
When the pods burst open,
the seeds are carried away
by the wind.

Milkweed grows
all over the country,
along roadsides
and in open sunny meadows.

INDIAN PIPE

Ghostly white "pipes"
stand on end
deep in the darkest woods.
People thought these looked
like peace pipes,
so they called this plant
Indian pipe.

Most plants get their energy
from the sun,
but Indian pipe lives
on the dead leaves and fungus
of the forest floor.
Because it does not need
sunlight, this plant can grow
where other plants
can't.

PITCHER PLANT

The pitcher plant
has leaves that are
shaped like a water pitcher.
Insects get trapped
inside the leaves.
They drown in the water
the leaves hold.
Then the pitcher plant
uses the insects for food!
This strange plant grows
where many other plants can't.
It does not need
sunlight or fresh air.
It lives off insects instead.

DUTCHMAN'S BREECHES

These white and yellow flowers
are strung all in a row,
like clothes on a line.
They are called
Dutchman's breeches
because they look like
tiny baggy trousers.

Insects with long tongues
reach up inside the flowers
to get the nectar
found inside.
Sometimes bees get there first.
They drill holes
in the tops of the flowers
and suck the nectar out.
Dutchman's breeches are found
deep in the cool, shady woods.

INDIAN PAINTBRUSH

The Indian paintbrush
has petal-like leaves
that cover the tiny flowers.
The leaves look as if
they were dipped in red paint.
Indians used the paintbrush
for medicine and for food.
Hummingbirds and bees
feed on the nectar
of this pretty red plant.
It grows in the open meadows
of the Western plains.

Skunk Cabbage

Skunk cabbage
was named for what it does.
It stinks!
This plant is one of the first
to start growing
in the spring.
You may see
and even smell
its cabbage-like leaves
as they poke through the snow.

Skunk cabbage can be found
along streams and
in wet places in the woods.

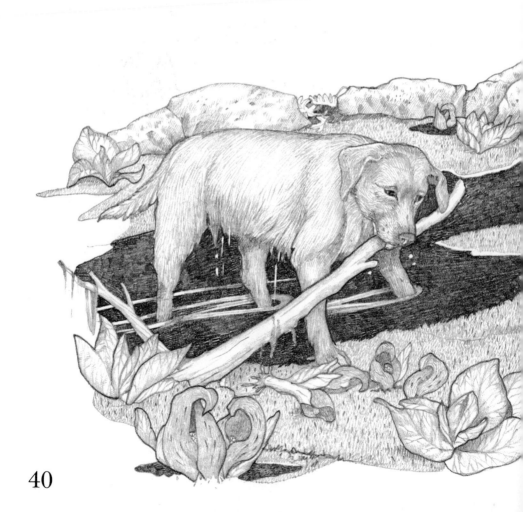

TOUCH-ME-NOT

Touch-me-not is also named
for what it does.
Just touch
these orange or yellow flowers
and the seeds come
flying out!
This is how touch-me-not spreads.

43

Its seeds are scattered
by birds and bugs.
In fact, anything
that brushes against it
helps this flower to spread.
It grows in fields
and along roadsides
all over the country.

Marsh Mallow

There are many
kinds of mallow plants.
One is called the swamp mallow.
Another is the rose mallow.
A third one,
with large, velvety leaves,
is the marsh mallow.
Its thick, gummy roots
made this plant famous.
Can you guess
what was made from them?
Marshmallows—the kind you roast.
Marsh mallow plants
can still be found
in salt- and fresh-water marshes
in the eastern United States.

We have seen many plants
with funny names.
There are many more.
See if you can guess
the reasons for
these plant names:
Turtlehead
Butter and eggs
Queen Anne's lace
Black-eyed Susan